MELANESIA AND LAND

ARON TAMBALA HEKENAI

PARTRIDGE

To order additional copies of this book, contact
Toll Free 800 101 2657 (Singapore)
Toll Free 1 800 81 7340 (Malaysia)
orders.singapore@partridgepublishing.com

www.partridgepublishing.com/singapore

CONTENTS

INTRODUCTION

The book tells about the experiences of the Melanesian people, a group who have lived in New Guinea for fifty thousand years ago. In this work of fiction, the main character reveals the changes that came from growing up in a nomadic lifestyle to settlement establishment and finally to a land occupation period. Land ownership, the primary focus of the book, explains the nature and principles applied to be coming landowners and that shape the identity of a Melanesian. It is hoped this book helps the younger generation understand the primary principles of rightful traditional landownership.

My aim is to educate future Melanesian generations about the principles practiced by their ancestors during the settlement period, when they transitioned from being hunters and gatherers to becoming landowners.

FIRST LIFE EXPERIENCES

Early Melanesians were victims of their living conditions; they distinguished between life and death for inhabitants. The stronger the people, the longer they lived. They became the forebears of today's Melanesian people.

Nature provided everything people needed to sustain life. But the ability to stand against extreme difficulties was impossible for some people. I was fortunate to have survived to this day to tell the account of these happenings; in particular, how the Melanesians shared the barren land they call their land.

My recounting unfolds with the happening of my birth and continues with my experiences as a wanderer and food gatherer. I then share life during the massive travelling revolution, settlement and landmark to home establishment and land portion sharing. I also explain the customary laws and guidelines pertaining to landownership in traditional Melanesia.

BIRTH AND CHILDHOOD IN THE WILDERNESS

Amid the trees and overgrown bushes of a tropical rainforest, and with wild animals watching, I was born to a family living in a cave-like shelter naturally built from rocks. As my parents would recall, all creatures of the universe were there to welcome me into the kingdom. The insects were seen in large numbers. The birds flew low, snakes hissed and crawled nearby, pigs and other four-legged animals were heard from mountaintops and from down in the valleys. My parents described this as unusual. They thought the spirits of deceased ancestors welcomed me. Or the animals mistook a human creature from an animal-like being.

An experience of a human baby in the bush was not a mistake. My first day on earth was celebrated by a buzzing mosquito band playing a jungle music titled "Buzz, Buzz, Buzz." They sang lullaby songs of welcome:"Welcome, our dear baby, we are utmost happy to have you in this world that we can feed on. We will welcome you with a bite each to taste the sweetness of your blood. Welcome, baby. Have a nice sleep, and we'll feed on you." When Mum noticed such a large number of mosquitoes, she builta fire to draw them away. But they accompanied my parents till daybreak.

Father gave me the name Waresu, with the nickname Bush. I did not know until later why he chose those names. I discovered that his parents once fed on breadfruit as stable food, and it brought him to manhood. "Ware" meant breadfruit. And he nicknamed me Bush because that was where I would grow up.

My father was 2.5 metres tall and weighed about 120 kilograms. His features had human and animal characteristics. Perhaps this was why wild animals came to see me when I was born. My mother was about 1.8 metres tall and slim. I was the eldest child. A sister, Mainalo, and a younger brother, Mosong, joined the family some years later.

Before my siblings arrived, I grew up with my parents in a cave. I learned the names of animals, plants, trees, insects, and all things in my environment. I ate fruit, meat, plant leaves, roots, and insects. Daddy climbed trees to pick fruit and collected eggs from nests for dinner. He hunted alone and caught animals for meat. Catching larger animals was more difficult than smaller ones, such as birds, bandicoot, grubs, and caterpillars. Mummy cooked or roasted them for dinner. I grew up very healthy and strong.

In my early years of life on earth, I spent much of my time with Mother, helping her collect wood for fire and fetch water. The task I liked most was collecting and preparing mud to make clay pots. When Mother decided to undertake the task, she unceasingly asked me to collect the mud. Roasting meat and climbing trees to collect fruit and birds' eggs from their nests were other deeds I liked doing. I grew up in a society with no gardens or houses. And I had no friends, so I did a lot of time with my parents.

One time when Father returned from his usual hunting trip, I asked him to tell me the experience of a man as a hunter. At the age of five, I was curious about it. After he told me about his experiences, I told Father I wanted to go with him on his next hunting trip. He agreed but said we would not go too far from the settlement site, There were dangerous animals that could attack me, and Mother must not be alone.

The next day he took me to a hill few kilometres from the cave. From the hilltop I saw smoke in the far distance. "Who is making that fire?" I asked.

"Those are other people," he answered.

"What are they doing?"

"Just like you, your mother, and I stay here hunting and gathering food to live, they are doing the same," replied Papa.

Besides the smoke, I saw valleys, rivers, and other distant places. "Can we go over there?" I asked.

"Yes. We will when the fruit and other food here finishes. Not only that, but when you grow big and strong enough to help me fight against large animals and maybe other people if they see us in their location."

"Why would people fight us?"

"They might think we are spirits or don't want us there. There are many people like us moving about this land. We don't know each other. When we meet others, they can attack us as we may become enemies to them. We don't know them, and they don't know us."

"Are you going to attack someone who comes here?"

"Maybe not until he makes the first attempt. I don't like to fight other people. I need them to be with me to walk this large land together. When you grow up, you can't live alone. You need other people to live with. If we do meet some people, I will ask them to stay with us."

"Father, honestly, you are a nice man," I mumbled.

Father showed me the traps he constructed and told me how to build them. "There are different kinds of traps. Traps for catching larger animals are differently constructed from those used to catch smaller ones. I will teach you how to make them when you grow older," said Father.

"This is powerful. Who taught you these skills, Father?"

"Just as I am telling you and will teach you, my father taught me all skills I needed to survive in this world."

Trap for small animals

SHELTER

The shelters were temporary structures. They ranged from earthen caves to tree hollows and manually built huts made of tree leaves and twigs:

My first experience was living in a cave-like shelter built from a fig tree's roots. I was born in this shelter and lived in it until I was ten years old. My sister was born in the cave. When I grew up, I noticed how it was designed to be used as a shelter for many years. But I wasn't satisfied simply with that discovery. As usual, I asked, "Dad, how did you build this house?"

"The fig tree is traditionally believed to be dwarf's home. Dwarfs are invisible humanlike beings who live a nomadic life, like us. They have no garden but plenty of food and meat to eat. They live in caves and big trees, like this one."

"Did one of them live here before you built our house?"

"Sure, son. It is an interesting story. Mum and I came this direction from the hills where sun rises. We were collecting nuts from trees over there and sat under this fig tree. Evening approached, and we couldn't continue. So we decided to spend the night in the cave-like space provided by this fig tree. I quickly cut leaves and additional twigs and framed a shelter. When doing this, Mum was sitting alone, eating fruit and nuts from the day's gathering. A fresh eatable fruit fell from the tree, hitting her on her head. She picked it up and ate it. Later, another one came down. She picked it up and ate it too. Then two more came down. Mum looked up and saw a man. He was your size but had a long beard, and fur grew all over him. He was smiling at her. She called me over and pointed at where the man sat. I looked and looked but was unable to see him. Mama grabbed me by my hand and again pointed in his direction. But despite all attempts, I was still unable to see him. But to Mama, he was visible."

"Why couldn't you see him?"

"Your grandfather told me that dwarfs are visible to women but hide from men."

"Father, why do they do this?"

"They are scared men might attack them. I made sure my hunting was never done far away, and Mama was never alone. Many times I took her with me. But they did no harm to us till you were born. I made sure some meat from hunting was spared for them."

"How was this done?"

"When meat is slaughtered, most is roasted. But some with the bones are put in a separate parcel, and a blind statement is made to them before sleep: 'My friends, your share of the meat is here. Please do come and take it.' At dawn, none is left, which means they surely took the meat. We lived happily together until we moved to an earthly cave."

Another interesting discovery was learning tool-making skills. Tools were constructed from different materials, including stones, animal bones, and hardwoods. I often saw Mama and Papa use these tools in their work. It was hard work using them, but there was satisfaction after their usage.

Learning the skills was not just a matter of listening to parents. Actually doing it helped acquire better survival skills.

One evening Papa returned home with a pig on his back. I demanded stories about how he caught the animal. Mama yelled from the fireplace, telling me to let Daddy rest. I pulled away, and the next instruction came. "Get me a bamboo, please, "Mama said.

"Why should I?" I asked.

"Nice boy, we need a tool to cut this pig, and a bamboo becomes a sharp tool that cuts easily into flesh."

"Thank you, Mama. I shall get that done now." I rushed over to the nearby bushes and came back with a bamboo. Daddy sat and watched as Mama split the bamboo and prepared several cuttings with sharp edges. I stood watching as she used one to cut through the pig's belly. "Can I use one to cut the other side, Mama?"

"Be careful, son. This is very sharp, and you can cut yourself too, "she cautioned. I took a piece and started working on the meat, following Mama's and Daddy's instructions on how and where to cut. Before nightfall, I was done with the slaughtering and took all the meat for roasting to the fireplace.

After that day's work, I knew a bamboo was used as tool for meat slaughtering. Removing and dislocating animal bones were done solely by stone axes. Stones fashioned into axe shapes were used to cut through hard surfaces, peel tree bark, and as weapons. Animal bones were used as weapons and for craft work.

When I was ten, a sister was born to the family. She was named Mainalo. Thank God. Mother needed help, and there she was for her aid. This satisfied my wish in having someone to take my place in the house with Mama all the time so I could help Papa with the man's work. Now both Mama and Papa had a helper.

Sometimes Father took us travelling up and down mountains, into valleys, across rivers, and floating on rafts to nearby islands to find food. Where food was plentiful, we stay for weeks or months. For example, when huge animals were caught, we built a shelter and stayed there until the meat was finished. Then we returned to the cave. But other times, we travelled for days without food.

MY EXPERIENCES AS
A WANDERER AND
FOOD-GATHERER

When I grew older, I helped Father gather food and meat for the family. I often travelled to hunt for meat, but mainly I collected prey from Father's established traps and collected fruit from trees for the family.

One day Papa was sick with fever, and I had to go alone to check the traps. As usual, I followed the tracks leading to the traps. Down hills, mountainsides, and along riverbanks I walked, checking every trap set by Papa. I noticed a human footprint going in the direction of Papa's hunting site. The print indicated that the man walked downstream as shown on the sand along the riverbank. I thought, *Some people must have been here yesterday. Or maybe someone lives here. I should be careful. If they see me, that be the end of me, and Papa and Mama would see me no more, as Papa warned me sometime ago.*

With that in mind, I was scared but curious to see this person and his hideout. Sowith caution, I followed the print downstream. From a distance, I saw smoke from a fire. I crept slowly towards the scene to avoid being seen by these people. I followed the footprint up the hill and then down the hill, using the new set of tracks. I moved further through the bushes, and from there, I could see some huts and people. I crawled towards a huge tree to get a better view. I hid in the tall grasses under the tree. I looked around to make sure no one had seen me. Then I stood beneath the trees to get a better view. This time I saw many people and houses. Women were sitting, standing, and chatting near the fireplace, perhaps cooking food for the day. In the distance, some men were working on their tools. One man was walking around the site, and a huge dog walked beside him. I knew from my father's stories that dogs were dangerous animals; they kill and tear men apart. I hid under the tree, surrounded by tall grasses, and watched the people moving about.

About midday, I no longer saw the men. Perhaps they had gone hunting again, leaving the women and children in the hut built from tree branches and leaves from palm trees. I crept out of my hiding place and hurried home. When at distance, I was satisfied with the discovery and rushed home to tell Father. I ran down slopes, ran up hills, and jumped over rocks in the river. I walk up and down hills. Over creeks swaying across rivers I rushed. Sliding on wet logs and rocks I fell, and rolling down mountainsides I went. I landed on a huge rock and was knocked unconscious. There I slept, so hurt with bruises all over. *Thank God, at least I am safe,* I thought. I slowly got up and continued the journey home to my papa, mama, and baby sister.

Though exhausted, I rushed into the cave. Daddy, who was resting, saw I was also hurt.The nature I was in signalled him of danger, and he ran for his weapons. My father came out of the cave and stood with an axe and hunting spear.He demanded, "Why are you in such hurry, exhausted, and bruised? Were you chased by an animal or by some people?"

"No, no, please wait. There was nothing chasing me, but I ran because I saw some people living along the river on the other side of those mountains. They came to our hunting ground," I explained. "There were many of them. I saw them and ran away to tell you. There were many men, women, and children. Their house was different from ours. They built it from big timber post, and the roof was built from palm tree leaves. One man had a very big dog, and I was frightened it might tear me up as you once told me."

"Son, you were lucky indeed. Dogs have a strong sense of smell. They can smell someone new or a stranger and chase it until it catches and kills it. Or they bark and signal the master to catch the prey if it is an animal."

"Thank you, Father. This didn't happen to me, or I would have been killed."

"What else did you see?"

"They live in an open grassland area with no bushes nearby. I also saw them make big fires and roast meat. Women and children about my age were around the fireplace, joking, laughing, and playing."

"Okay. Sit down and have something to eat. And you can tell me more about your discovery."

Mama gave me some meat and gently spoke into my ear, "Be careful, boy. There are wild animals and people out there who will kill you."

"Thank you, Mama. I am safe; no one saw me." Papa said some magic needed to be given to me to call for supernatural help when such situations occurred."Right, Papa. I want us to go there one day and see them. Would you agree with this idea?" I asked.

Papa thought for a little while and then asked, "Why do you want us to go there?"

"Papa, I think living with other people is good. I saw many children about my age, and I want to play with them."

"Like I said, son, that's a great idea. But this will take time. I have to find out for myself who they are before we go any nearer. There is great risk in meeting someone you have not seen in life, and you can be mistaken for an animal and killed. What if I am killed? You are just a small boy who cannot support Mama and your sister. We will surely go there one day."

"Alright, Papa. Now I understand your reason." I sat quietly for some minutes and then called out, "Papa, I am sorry I didn't visit all the traps. Would you like to go and check them yourself?"

"No, son," he replied."I am sick and need rest. We have enough to eat for the week."

"Thank you, Papa. I need rest too. I'll sleep for a while and maybe talk to you later. "Bye."

While resting, I flew to the dream world. There I noticed a man, woman, and children swaying in the water. I wondered what they were doing and toddled nearer. At a closer look, I saw them gathering fish traps. They had caught fish in each of the traps they had in the river. *I wish I had a fish for dinner,* I thought, but I was scared to ask them. Having caught the fish, they walked ashore to where I was hiding. The woman came towards my hiding place to cut leaves. I thought, *They have discovered my hiding place,* so I ran away. She saw me and called to her husband, who chased me. But before he caught me, I screamed and woke up.

"Bush, just a short sleep and you screamed. Why?" Mama asked.

"Did I, Mama? I was chased by a man I saw today at the village. He saw me running and ran after me."

"Never go there again," said Mama.

"But I really want us to go and stay with them."

Some days later, Papa decided he and I should go to that village. As usual, he got his weapons, and off we went. Uphill and downhill we travelled. I slid on some wet rocks and fell. We walked down the river I saw in the dream. We waded across the river without difficulty.

On the beach where I saw the footprint we could see footprints of someone who just walked upstream too. Papa said we should sit there and wait for the man's return. "We can't walk into the village as strangers. We need someone to lead us," Papa explained. "Keep silent or they will see us."

"Okay, Papa. I promise to be a good boy and be quiet."

After a long hour of waiting, two men appeared. Papa hid behind a huge tree beside the track and told me to go further into the bush. As they walked past, Papa came from behind and grabbed the last man in line. He took the shooting position and held his spear toward the first man. Papa was just too big for the two men. He commanded them to be quiet or they would die. They obeyed. "Sorry, my friends. I don't mean any harm but wish to talk to you," Papa said. "Would you mind sparing some time with me before you go home?"

"Yes, yes we can," they both said nervously.

The men sat down together for a conversation. I walked out from my hiding place and joined them. Father introduced us to the strangers, and we greeted each other before our talk. Papa told them about our hideout and many more stories.

Finally, Papa asked them the question that I have always wished for. Papa started, "I noticed you live in big group in a village. My family and I live alone beyond those mountains. We wish to come and stay with you in the village. What would you or your people say about this proposal?"

"Great man, please do come. I agree and am sure everyone else will, including the village chief," said the first man nervously.

The second man added, "You are a huge man who can help us fight enemy travellers. Please come. We will go and tell everybody in the village."

They asked when we would be ready to move to the village. Papa replied, "Not until the chief is aware and agrees with the idea."

"We will tell the chief and later arrange for your coming," one of the men said. The first man said he would arrange for some men and women to come to our hideout and take our family over.

Papa nodded."That's a good idea, but would you know the way to my location? Before we depart, I'll show you the track to the site."

"That is a good idea, great man," the first man replied, and they followed. "By the way, what is your name?" one of them asked.

"I am Malaka," replied Papa."

"This means you are a big man?" one of the men asked.

"Yes. Maybe that was why my father gave me the name." They all laughed. Papa and I showed them the track to our site, said goodbye, and travelled home.

At home, I told Mama all that happened and the great news that we would be moving to join the people I saw and live with them in a village."How will I take all these things with Mainalo and walk that far?" Mama asked.

"Arrangements have been made. Men and women from that village will come to help us."

"When are they coming?"

"Papa will know the day, and he will inform us."

"Very well, son, I am happy too," said Mama and continued with her cooking duty.

Some days later, Papa said to mama and me, "The days are counting down, and the people will be coming to get us very soon. Please get some food ready for them, and we will go together." With that, we all got to work. I helped Mama cared for my sister, Mainalo, and she prepared food. Papa collected other things and tied them together.

An hour later, we heard people talking and walking down the hill to the cave."Hello, everyone. Thank you for coming. Please rest. When Mama is done with the food, you'll eat, and then we will be ready to leave." The villagers were surprised to see Mama was big and tall, like Papa. Mama greeted the visitors and arranged for the women's resting place while Papa helped with the men.

Mama prepared enough food for us all. I helped distribute the food. Everybody ate some meat with fruit and vegetables. After the meal, they helped carry all the household items, and off we moved to their village.

We travelled the whole day and eventually arrived before nightfall. The dogs, children, women, and men welcomed us to the village in their own ways. The dogs barked, the children stared and giggled, the women hugged, and the men sang. I ran behind Papa when I saw the dogs coming closer. "Don't be scared. They won't bite," he said."Maybe one day we will look after one as a pet ourselves." The village was light with laughter and happiness that evening.

We rested in the village chief's residence. The people of the village came to greet us with cooked food served in huge wooden bowls. After the meal, we spent the night in the chief's house.

The next morning, the village chief called a gathering of all the men and women. "Papa, what is that? It sounds like an animal's voice."

"It is a conch shell from the sea. It is used to send messages to people far away. Your grandfather had one, but it fell into the sea when the raft capsized while travelling to the mainland from an island," replied Papa.

"Wow, I wish I had one. Maybe when I grow older."

A conch shell

At daylight, I had a good look at the village. It was a long village with many houses. Papa was with the chief, so Mama, Mainalo, and I walked about the village led by a woman who talked a lot. She introduced us to everyone we passed. I saw many children my age looking at me. I knew I would have many colleagues to play with.

We walked to one end of the village and noticed a new house. "Who lives in that house?" I asked the village woman.

"No one. It is new, just built over a week ago."

"Wow, that looks beautiful," I said, and we continued walking.

From there we moved over to the crowd that was waiting for the chief and the big men of the village. We greeted each other and met new friends while waiting.

Not long after we got there, the chief and his men walked out of their meetinghouse. Papa was with them but walked behind. "Hi, everyone," greeted the chief. "The purpose of the day's gathering is to introduce to you a new member of our village family. This great man is Malaka. His wife is Wamatakuwa. Their handsome son is Bush, and the baby is Mainalo. Malaka is a member of Muruk tribe. Coincidently, he joined the right tribe here." The crowd cheered. "This is a village of the Muruk tribe. I welcome you on behalf of my people as the appointed chief. Before other talks, I wish to have you settled today. The village welcomes you with a house to live in. Please lead our new member to his house," concluded the chief.

Some men lead Papa to the house I'd noticed earlier. "Malaka, this is your house" said the old man in the group.

"Thank you, everyone," Papa said.

Most of the others left, but the women and girls helped move our things over to the new house. We settled in, and life in the village began.

NEW CHIEF

In some years of living together, the chief led the village men in doing many things, including building houses, participating in rituals, hunting, and fighting in battle against travelling warriors. All the men admired Papa's participation. Because of his muscular build, all tasks were easy.

One evening in the rest house, Lapun, the village chief, told his men, "Fellow men, I feel time has come to transfer the chief title to another person for age has caught up with me."

Papa intervened, "You have done so well in looking after the tribe. I have received the best honour as a stranger coming into an established village during the wandering period of the primitive life."

"Thank you, Malaka. You have contributed well in maintaining the tribe. I see you have great potential and will give you the responsibility of the chief title after informing the rest of the men."

"Me? No, no, let the people select, " Papa begged.

"Malaka, I can make the decision. Gentlemen, it is clear that someone will need to replace me. I have little time and will set the time for this appointment. Before that day comes, you need to look among yourselves and suggest someone to succeed my position." The idea of having Papa as chief was first among all the men.

Finally, the day came for the new village chief to be appointed. All men were in the resting house, and the discussion began with the chief in lead. "Any nominations for the chief's position?" asked Lapun. One in the group stood and nominated Papa. "Any others to be nominated?" Lapun asked.

One of the men responded,"Lapun, I think Malaka is enough. I asked that we close the nominations." Everyone agreed. Lapun walked over to Malaka and hugged him, a gesture of blessing. He handed the conch shell and other secret material to Malaka as the new chief.

Garamut drums were beat, and the conch shell was blown. Women and children in their houses heard men singing in the distance."Why are the men singing and playing drums at this unusual time?" asked one of the talkative women.

"A new chief is appointed in place of Lapun," said a man just walking out of his house.

"Who is the new chief?" asked the woman, running over to his house.

"You guess," said the man.

"Is it Kella?"

"No, dear."

"Is it Wako?" The woman guessed again.

"No, dear."

"Is it Sikau?"

"No," was again was the man's answer.

"Then is it Malaka?"

"Yes," answered the man. The women danced at the great news.

The news of the new chief's appointment moved from one household to another. Mothers and children came to congratulate the new chief with laughter, singing, and dancing. The night's long feast of pig roasting and cooking of other food continued till daybreak in celebration of the appointment.

Papa became the village chief from then on.

My wish to live in the village with many people was fulfilled. I had many friends to play with, and Papa had a larger fighting force to defend us against enemy warriors.

MYSTERY

Living together with other people was worthy. People depended on each other for survival. Each season meant certain activities. For example, the wet season was suitable for pig hunting. The dry season was for extensive hunting in the bush by men and women. Men hunted for tree kangaroos, cuscus, pigs, cassowaries, and birds. Men and women fished. Near the village, rivers flowed from hilltops to the sea and lakes. These rivers had plenty of fish which attracted women to be in the river on dry, sunny, hot days.

Individuals were banned from fishing in Falaka Lake for years. But as time passed, the idea to harvest the fish in the lake came to the village people's mind, in particular the women's. They decided the fish had multiplied so much, and fishing would bring a good harvest. Tawayekle, the talkative lady, nicknamed Mauswara, initiated the that fishing be allowed in Falaka Lake this season.

She moved through the village, from one end to the other, inviting the women and girls to go fishing that very day. "I am going fishing today, and I invite all women and young girls to follow me. Falaka Lake, next to the cliff, has not been fished for the last years, and there are plenty of fish. Today we will catch fish, turtles, eels, and even crocodiles. Get some food to cook for lunch."

"How do you know there are plenty of fish, Mauswara?" asked Kella, a talkative male.

"Ha, ha, ha. You aren't a woman, my friend. You go hunting in the bushes and know where pigs can be found. But you know nothing about what's in the river and lakes. Tell your wife to follow me, and you will eat fish this evening," demanded Tawayekle.

"Okay, Mauswara," answered Kella as he chewed betelnuts and walked away.

"Hey, Kella, you have not answered my question. Is your wife coming with me?" asked Mauswara from behind.

"Yes, Mauswara, your friend will follow you. I will wait to see you all home with fish in large containers and eat the largest fish," responded Kella. And he walked off to tell his wife.

A moment later, the village women, children, and men gathered around for a discussion led by Mauswara. "Good morning, I have an idea to fish in the Falaka Lake today. The lake is shallow and has lots of fish. Before the season changes and the rain falls, we need to catch all these fish."

"How will these be done?" asked a woman from the crowd.

"Toxic substances from plants will be used to kill the fish," explained Mauswara. "All the women need fishing spears and nets to catch the fish when they float on the surface."

A man stood and asked Mauswara, "What if a crocodile comes out and kills one of you, let me say, kills my wife?"

"I will give you a young girl as a new wife," was Mauswara's response, bringing the crowd to laughter.

Soon after the discussion, the women gathered their fishing gear and set off for the lake.

At the lake, the women prepared the toxic plant roots. Mauswara announced, "One hour will be given for the process. After this, I will give a countdown for all women to pour the substance into the lake. Do you hear me?"

"Yes, yes, yes, yes, yes," answered the women sitting around the lake.

A little while later, Mauswara called again. "Ready," she count, "five, four, three, two, one, go" In under a second, all the prepared substance extracted from the toxic plants went flying into the lake. The women cleaned themselves of the poisonous substance. Some helped themselves to rolls of tobacco and betelnuts while waiting for the substance to work in the lake.

Meanwhile, the lake's fish population noticed some unusual signs. The water was cloudy and smoky-looking. They wondered what was happening. The elder fish quickly called out, "A chemical been used against us. In the past, most of the fish died. Very few survived to bring about this new population."

Just as it finished talking, there was screaming in one corner of the lake. The great eel called out, "Many of us will die as the result of this activity. Please listen, everybody. The water is poisoned, and we have very little chance of survival."

"What can we do?" asked a fish.

"There is one possibility. You dive and make your way into the mud, where the poisoned water will not go through. There is no choice. Feed on the mud for two or three days. Those who wish to survive take this option. Those who wish to die because your family members died, make that choice. There is very little chance for our survival."

Crying and shouting came from all over the lake. Fish were dying every second. Their movements caused waves that grew beyond the banks. "We have always become victims of this human feeding activity. We need to fight back," said the larger fish. The great fish, the biggest crocodile, the tortoise, and other huge fishlike creatures of the lake got together at one corner of the lake and discussed the nature of the revenge battle which would be led by the great eel.

The largest crocodile said, "Crocodiles will survive this disaster. We can live on water and land. We will go and chase all the women up there and kill them all."

"But men are cleverer than us. They have huge spears and will kill all of you," said the great eel.

"Yes, that is correct. The men are still the strongest," said one fish.

"Then what is the next option?" asked the great eel. Everyone was silent. "Don't you have another good idea?" Still, no one said a word. The great eel spoke louder this time. "There is no time for further talk. I can feel the toxic substance in the water affecting my eyes now .And in the next minutes, it will affect my whole body system, and will die. I will die for you all. We are powerful creatures, and this I will do to fight back for you all."

"Please talk quickly. I can't stand this condition. I need to hide," said a fish.

"Okay, I will die with the fish that are already dying. When the humans have eaten my meat, my spirit will destroy them tonight. Send all the spirits we have in this lake to come through the rain, wind, lightning, and we will fight the human creatures. Will you help me with this idea?" the great eel asked.

"Yes, yes, yes," replied the fish.

"Go," the great eel commanded, and everyone sought refuge in safe, deep, muddy spots in the lake.

As the women were collecting, catching, and killing unconscious fish, filling their baskets, Mauswara walked from one corner of the lake to the other, ensuring every woman had enough fish for themselves. The catch was a great success. Baskets were almost full, and there were no more fish on the surface. The women gathered to prepare the fish for home when the great eel was seen floating. "Hooray, another fish for us," they went into the lake and dragged the huge eel out of the water.

"Hurry, hurry! We need to cut this huge eel before dark," said Mauswara.

Moment later, someone called, "Mauswara, the eel has been cut. Please help distribute the meat equally to us." Mauswara walked over, puffing her tobacco, and distributed the meat among the women. The head was given to Mama as the village chief's wife. Their baskets now full and the sun setting low, they left the lake for their homes. Eagerly anticipating the meals their husbands prepared in the women's absence.

Mauswara told everyone to walk together. Just before they entered the village, she told them to sing a song of successful hunting.

"Hooray, hooray," the women shouted. Alarmed, the men and children ran out of their houses to meet their mothers and sisters.

There was laughter, joy, and excitement in the village. Every house had a roasting bed with fish drying. The children played hide-and-seek in the clear moonlight, and the men chatted and sang in the rest house. The hard day of work sent some women straight to bed, leaving the roasting duties to their children and husbands. Some went to bed after dinner while others helped their husbands and children roast fish all night.

After dinner, I helped Papa roast the fish Mama brought. First, Papa and I counted the fish. And to our surprise, there was the eel's head. "Hey, Papa, there's snake in the basket," I screamed and jumped away.

"That's an eel's head." I demanded an explanation. Papa quickly responded, "An eel is a snake-like fish. It lives in water or a river like all other fish. It is big and long as some snakes, but it has nostrils and tails like fish. Its meat is oily."

"Okay, Papa, I will eat its head after it is roasted," Mama called out from her resting place. "Bush, Bush, I wish to tell you how the eel was caught. But please give me time to sleep, I am very tired and need rest."

"Thank you, Mama. I will be prepared for you tomorrow. Bye, ayo, Mama."

Mama was tired, so went to sleep early. Papa and I roasted the fish for the family and went to sleep very late at night.

The next morning, everyone in the village talked about the great fishing trip the mothers and the girls made the day before, the excitement of the event and their good catch. Mauswara, as usual, walked the village from end to end, cheering people and chewing and smoking her rolled tobacco. Near Kella's house she called, "Kella, your wife came back safe from crocodile attack. You will need to eat the eel meat I gave her yesterday and make more jokes like the fish in the lake." She laughed.

Meanwhile, in the lake, the other fish came out of their hiding places in the mud. They found almost everyone in the community dead; there were no remains of them around the lake, even at the surface. They also noticed the great eel was missing. Then they remembered his words that he was to die for them on the condition that they help him destroy the human inhabitants. The survivors gathered for the release of the spirits of the lake the next day.

Not knowing the fish's plan, the people set a feast to celebrate the successful fishing the women had the day before. The men practiced songs for the sing-sing (dance), while women and children prepared food in their houses.

In the evening the feast started. The men played the drums and sang songs. The women danced joyfully to the rhythm of the music.

The early part of the evening brought bright moonlight and stars shining in the sky. I noticed the event to be very unique and said to Mama and Papa, "I have not seen a large catch and a feast made in celebration of this kind since we came here. This is the first of its kind."

Papa replied, "Yes, son, you are not wrong. But once in a while, this does happen, and you should experience it."

"Thank you, Papa. I have learned something new in life."

I went to the dancing arena and joined other children. We danced to the music played by our papas and uncles. Vocal Mauswara was the highlight of the women in the village. She received praise and credit from both men and women for her leadership.

THE STRANGE NIGHT

At almost midnight, the lighting from the moon and the stars suddenly changed. The moon and stars shone dimmer and dimmer, until their light disappeared. Total darkness grew, shadowing the area. Thunder sounded in distance. Some people continued dancing, but many took shelter in their houses. Then the situation got worse. The area grew very dark. There were strong lightning strikes, and loud thunder rumbled down on the village. Heavy rain started falling, and those who had remained at the festivities ran for their houses.

Beneath the storm, the spirits flew above the village to take revenge on the people."Ha, ha.Goodnight human beings. You had your time to kill the fish, and now it is my turn to take revenge on you all. Ha, ha," said the spirit of the lake. "I will kill you all! Get prepared, my friends, I am coming, I am coming, I am coming. Ha, ha, ha!"

The spirit, flying in the dark, ordered, "Let the lightning strike the village." And it obeyed, striking and striping the tall trees and forcing them to fall over on to some houses. People inside screamed and ran to another house. The spirit continued, "Let heavy rain fall in this village." And the falling raindrops were as hard as stones. Water in creeks, rivers, and drains increased in volume.

I called to Mama and Papa, "The storm is unusual. Could it be caused by some spirits? Mama, would it be the spirits from the lake?"

"Son, I think you are right," replied Mama. "The eel we caught was the largest I have ever seen, and a storm of this nature is not wrong with your suggestion."

Papa explained, "Spirits live in huge animals and trees. They have extreme supernatural powers over human beings and the environment. When they are attacked or disturbed, they destroy anything and everything around and within their target zone. For this reason, I think the spirit of the fish and the eel the mothers caught are here for revenge."

"How do we help ourselves. Can we see them and fight too?"

"No, son, you can't see the spirits. And you can't fight them either."

"What do we do now, Papa? The storm is so strong."

Papa was troubled. "Where is the eel's head?" he asked.

"It is in the basket," I answered.

"Please bring it over to me."

I quickly took the basket and searched for the eel's head. I used a flame produced from the bamboo torch as a light.

"Wait. The whole village is screaming. Something terrible must have happened to them." I gave the head to Papa and rushed out of the house. Papa followed.

The wind was so strong, the rain was very heavy, and the night was so dark that a person standing a meter away could not be seen. Lightning flashed violently, and the thunder sounded fiercely. A cyclone had hit the village dangerously hard. Papa held me tightly against the wind. I looked through the lightning and saw the neighbors' houses being destroyed. "Papa, the houses are broken. Where are the people?"

"Bush, let us turn back. This looks very dangerous," Papa replied. We walked, guided by the flashes of lightning. The second house was also gone. And people were nowhere to be seen. "Bush," Papa called, "we need to turn back to the house, or our house may be destroyed and Mama and your sister killed while we were out. Come on. Hurry up, boy."

Papa and I hurried back to the house, barely missing flying tree branches and falling trees and building materials from destroyed houses. We rushed back to the house. "Mama, Mama," I called.

"Why are you yelling, Bush?"

"Sorry, I pleaded. Where is Mainalo?"

"Son, we are both here."

"Mama, there is bad news. Papa and I walked a few metres away from our house and noticed our neighbors' houses totally destroyed, and they were nowhere to be seen. They may have been killed or blown away by the wind."

I explained further."Papa and I moved further and noticed a similar situations and returned."

"Bush, there is nothing much you and Papa can do. Please sit down. And pray to your ancestors to save us from this angry cyclone belhat."

"Why call the cyclone 'belhat'?" I asked because it was a new word.

"When it started, we discussed spirits and powers and revenge. This was a storm created by the spirits of the lake in revenge for the killing of many fish, including the giant eel. I had its head."

"How do you know it is really from the spirits of the lake, Mama?"

"When you and Papa left the house, I prayed to my ancestral spirits. And I found myself standing outside our house and heard some angry men shouting at the end of the village."

"What did they say?" I asked.

"They said, 'Ha, ha, you hungry human beings. You destroyed my village and killed everybody. I am here to take revenge. Come out of your house and fight. Now I will take all your lives tonight, and you will no longer live here to destroy my world. Ha, ha.' And then, It said, "Where is my head? I want my head. 'I knew I had the eel's head. With fright, I woke up just before you and Papa came back."

Papa heard what Mama said and asked for the eel's head. I took it from the basket and gave it to him. He grabbed hold of the head and ran out. Standing in the dark, rainy, and stormy night, Papa shouted at the top of his voice, "You had revenge on my people. I wish you were men, so we could see each other and talk. You have destroyed my village. Come and take your head, and leave us alone!" Papa threw the eel's head into the strong wind moving towards him.

The strong wind lessened, and the rain fell more lightly. And the lightning and the thunder faded away.

"Now I believe that spirits have power to destroy," I told Mama, Papa, and Mainalo.

"You all need rest. Please go to sleep. We will inspect the village tomorrow to see the damage done," said Papa. The remaining night brought fitful rest till daybreak.

I was anxious to discover the damage the next morning, so I woke up early, even before Papa, Mama, and Mainalo. I walked out of the house, and to my surprise, the village was deserted. There were no houses. The tall trees and coconuts had all fallen to earth and were lying everywhere. I ran into the house and woke everyone.

"Bush, don't disturb Papa. He is tired" called Mainalo.

Papa heard us talking and woke up. Mama also awoke, and they walked out of the house. I grabbed Papa's hand, and Mama held Mainalo as we walked the empty village. All houses were pulled down. Some even had materials removed from their sites. "Why are we the only family to survive this cyclone?" I asked. Papa didn't answer. "What do you think, Mama?" Mama too didn't answer.

Papa and Mama were very puzzled and wondered what happened to all the people. There were no dead bodies or survivors on the scene. "Where could they have gone? Did the wind sweep them all into the lake? Did the wind blow them all to distant places?"

All my questions went unanswered by the family. Mama tried to explain. "We didn't eat the eel. That is maybe why we weren't hit by the storm."

"Maybe," replied Papa.

Papa was confused and kept quiet all day. He was perhaps wondering why this disaster occurred, why he was left unhurt. And more important, where were all the people? Were they hurt, dead, or alive?

Papa sent Mama and Mainalo to prepare breakfast. He asked me to help search the village for any bodies. But after hours of searching, we found no bodies—human or domesticated animals, like dogs and pigs. "Papa," I called, "I can't see any remains of men or animal in my search."

"Okay, come back. We'll wait and see what happens tomorrow. Go back to the house, and have something to eat."

The mystery of what happened to the villagers remained unsolved.

The village was my home for the rest of my life. A brother was born into the family and was named Mosong, bringing the total of family members to five, two boys, a girl, and our parents. We lived alone in the village for some years.

THE TRAVELING AND
SEVERE RIOTING PERIOD

I had no choice for I had no friends. I went nowhere for I had no friends. I told no more stories or jokes for I had no friends. I had no choice but to be alone.

I had no one to play with. I sometimes walked about the village, recalling their names and our past doings. In imaginary situations, I shouted their names but was heard by no one. "Who will go with me to the river?" No one answered. "Who will go hunting with me?" Still no one answered. I had no choice, but Papa became a friend.

I also noticed Papa's loneliness. There were no men around to chat with or discuss the important issues of the village. He discussed matters with Mama and needed me on his hunting trips. Mainalo helped Mama, cared for Mosong, and did the housework. Life continued this way for many years in the village of a single family.

One day Papa said, "We can't move anymore; we will live here forever. But all my men are lost, and I need to be extra strong to defend us incase other people come our way. I will need to walk frequently to the land we used for hunting. There is a chance other travelling tribes will claim it after making an establishment on it. Bush, you are in your teenage, and I will need your help to get this task done."

"That shall be done, Papa." To his surprise I was growing to his giant physical size.

Early the next morning, Papa said, "We can't wait any longer. We will have to start this week. A week before the disaster, my men and I were out hunting over those hills and caught sight of other groups of men. They were also armed and walking about the hillside. But we chased them over hills further away."

"Why did you chase them?" I asked.

"Bush, they almost killed your talkative uncle Kella. They missed him with an arrow, and we reacted."

"Why didn't you let the children and mothers know of that event?"

"You could be scared, that's why. Our principal role as father and man is to protect the children and women as much as possible. This is what you will do when you grow older. You will join your tribesmen and fight against any approaching tribal groups.

"Go to sleep early. We need to go to those mountaintops to ensure no travelling tribe settles there. That's the furthest our men walked during hunting. It is our land territory," said Papa.

Just before dawn, I woke up and prepared my gear, including weapons, food, and a coat. "Bush," called Papa.

"Yes, Papa. I am ready."

"Let's go," said Papa, and my training to be a warrior started on that trip.

We left the village when the second rays of sunlight drew into the village, breaking its darkness. "We need to be back quickly. Mama and the kids will be alone," said Papa, and we rushed off into the bush.

We climbed up and down hills and followed rivers and streams. We walked along ridges. At one place we stopped, and Papa told me the names of rivers, creeks, and many sections of land explored. "Where did you get these names from?" I asked.

"When events occur on sites as this, the location deserves the name of perhaps people or animals involved in the occurrence. This has helped in keeping records of happenings.

"The creek below is named Kella bun; 'bun' means 'bone'. This was named after Kella, who hurt his backbone when he slip off the cliff and fell into the pool below when we were chasing a pig."

"Wow. Very sorry, Uncle Kella," I said.

"Ya. Uncle Kella was talkative and kept most men laughing with his jokes. I am sorry he is gone somewhere," mumbled Papa to himself.

"This land is named Wasko—spirits' home. The place was named after a man was chased by spirits.

"And Papa, what is the river down in the valley called?"

"Son, that is call Fly River for it flows so fast. It can quickly drag and pull you downstream, and you can get drowned."

"Please, can we go there?"

"Yes, but not now."

We moved a little further, and another question flew out of my mouth."Papa, that mountain is so high. What would you call it?"

"That is call Mountain fire after fire, stones and ashes came from that mountain and killed all animals and plants under it."

Papa continued, "As I mentioned earlier, the names for land areas are usually of animals, people, trees and events that were found there and need to be remembered. You can name some places later in your life that can be remembered by the next generation."

"Thank you, I have learnt a lot on this trip."

By midday, we reached our destination. Papa planted some tanget and we turned back.

"There is other knowledge you must learn," he said.

"What is it, Papa?"

"This is the knowledge on how to divide land with neighboring clans and tribes. Some days later others will come to stay with you."

"Okay, what do I need to know?"

He showed me the ridge we walked on and said, "Ridges, hilltops and mountain tops are good natural features and be used to mark land boundaries of two tribes. The first owns one side, the second owns the other. The ridge remains a good boundary indicator.

"Besides the ridge, are creeks and rivers. They divide land to two sides too. When rivers and creeks aren't at reachable distances, large trees, plants, and stones be used to show divisions and separations. And the sea areas are marked using points, reefs and huge rocks."

"Thank you. I know how to help share land for two or more groups."

With Papa teaching me these traditional principles of landmarks and identification, the trip seemed quite short. Before I realised it, Papa said we were nearly home. "Wow, Papa, that was fast, wasn't it?" I said.

"Yes, but before we go to the house, there is one more thing we have to do. Let us inspect the traps your uncles and

I set." Before long, we noticed all the traps had done their job in catching what they were intended for. We collected ten bandicoots, twenty birds, some lizards, and a kangaroo.

"This is too much for a day. Hope we won't have another cyclone belhat."

"No, no. That won't happen. Wrap them up in these leaves. We ought to be home before dark. Mama will need to prepare them for cooking." I got things done as instructed, and we walked home.

Almost home, I called, "Mama, Mama, please come and help me!" Mama and Mainalo ran out of the house and hugged me. They removed the load from my shoulders and took it to the house. Papa added his load too. And to Mama's surprise, there was plenty of meat for the family.

Papa and I had dinner early and went to bed. I mumbled to myself, "This is what it means to be a man. And with the day's tasks, I need good rest." I fell asleep while Mama and Mainalo cut and roasted the day's collection.

Journey with father

MEETING OTHER PEOPLE

A month later, Papa decided to go hunting."How far will we go this time, Papa?"

"As far as Kella Creek. We need to reconstruct the traps."

"Do I carry my weapons?"

"Yes, son. You must remember one thing. We are living in a wildlife period. You can be attacked by other people or wild animals at any time. Whether you are in the village or in the bush, your weapons must be in easy reach." Papa paused before continuing."The nomadic life has ended, and people are moving to new sites to make permanent settlement, like we did. These people travel in large groups and fight their way through. If we aren't prepared, one of these groups can kill us and take our possessions, including the land."

"Okay, you need to teach me to fight using these weapons."

"Yes, son, that will be done next time around. Perhaps next week," said Papa.

I rushed to the first row of traps and found them all down, lying ideal. I worked on the first one, cutting new vines and twigs and placing bait. I moved to the next and next until they were all done. Papa maintained and set the second row of traps in catching position.

After a long day of hard, dirty work, we toddled down to the Kella rivulet to wash. I jumped into the pool and right beneath the water, enjoying its coolness. "Papa, come down and wash too," I called.

"No, not yet, Bush. After you finish and take guard.

"Why, Papa?"

"When you wash, I provide you security. Son, you understand?"

"Yes." I cleaned myself hurriedly and got out of the water that Papa could have his turn.

As I walked off the beach, Papa whispered from behind, "Hurry up, grab your spear. People are coming our way." I got hold of my spear and shield. "Since you are right-handed, hold your shield tied on your left and the spear on the right. And sit behind me."

I was scared, my legs quaked, I was shivering as sweat dripped down my forehead. "We will take them by surprise, and they won't attack. Remember my word. I don't fight and kill others until they cause it to happen." I moved a little further away from Papa to get a better view. In the distance, I could see two elderly men, two youth about my age, a little girl about Mainalo's age, and two women of Mama's age. "Shhh, keep quiet. They are coming closer." Papa warned me not to stare at a stranger from a hiding position for they will locate me. I remembered these words.

Closer and closer they came. Papa sat still, allowing them to pass, and would attack from behind. As they came to our hideout, they noticed our footprints and were alarmed to take extra care.

Just before the next word, Papa jumped out of the hiding and polked the man with the spear. Papa was very tall and strong. The opponent was smaller. It was no match; Papa would always win. The travellers mean no harm in revenge and quickly surrendered. "I am very sorry coming into your territory. We're fleeing a raid in a settlement many days' walk from here. Please, are you going to kill us?" the man asked.

"No, I won't. But I will take you home, and we will discuss that later," Papa said.

"Thank you. Let me introduce the family. I am Hunganambel, and that is my wife, Suwala. This is Wanebangau, his wife, two sons, and daughter. We belong to the Muruk tribe."

Papa wasn't surprised because he was also member of Muruk tribe. "Okay, we'll get to know each other in our discussion. We need to move. Bush lead these people home."

Just before walking on, Papa asked the traveller if anyone was chasing them. "No, great man, no enemy is behind us. Thank you for the nice welcome," said Hunganambel, and we walked home.

Papa has exposed me to a good experience, I though as I led them home. Papa followed from behind,

Approaching the village, I called, "Mama, Mama, I have some new friends with me come and meet them please."

She stood and watched curiously as we walked to the house. "Hellow," she greeted the visitors and seated them on palm mats. They introduced themselves to Mama, Mainalo, and Mosong. When Papa arrived, Mama left to prepare dinner for the family and the visitors.

I was listening to my new friends talking about their adventure when my father called, "Bush, Mama needs help with dinner preparation. Excuse yourself and assist Mama first."

"Okay, Papa." I replied. I went into the house and helped Mama. She prepared sago, and I cooked meat. Before dark, dinner was served, and everyone's hunger was satisfied.

Straight after dinner, the room was organized and space prepared for the travelling visitors. Nothing much was shared that evening since the visitors were tired, and most of us went to bed early. Papa and Hunganambel stayed up for some hours and went to sleep later.

ACCOUNT OF EARLY MIGRATION AND SETTLEMENT

The next morning, we were curious to hear stories happening in distant places from our visitors. Papa stood and said, "I wish to welcome my fellow tribesman Hunganambel, your wife, and family members to my village. We were with a big tribe of men, women, and lots of children, but they are here no more. A storm that I called cyclone belhat occurred few years ago and swept them all off. Their disappearance is still a mystery today. My family was the only one left untouched. We are alone. I understand that you are a member of Muruk tribe. Before you tell us of your escape and happenings in far distant places, I wish to ask you of your destination point and if you would you prefer stay with me and my family here."

Hunguanambel stood and responded, "There is no man on earth who treat strangers with such warm hospitality. You are a great man. As today's life is concerned, people gather around in tribal groupings and protect themselves, families, and land. You are a great man indeed; I have no destination point of travel as we were forced to run away from frequent fights we had with many other travelling tribes. The recent fight had many people killed. I ran away, taking all my family. I do not think of continuing but wish to stay here with you forever and give you additional strength in defending against rival warriors should they come this way."

Papa couldn't hold back his excitement. He walked over and hugged his new fellow tribesman as a symbolic sign of agreement. Everybody cheered. Papa spoke more boldly, "You will all live with me in my house until your new houses are built."

The younger brother stood and told his account of the fleeing. "Out there, migrations of tribal groups move almost every month through our previous settlement site. Some pass the village without a fight and continue to distance places; others decide to fight with us and take our place. On several occasions we won the fight and chased them. But the recent group was too much, and couldn't stand against them. There was the option of running away or to fight and die. My elder brother and I run away, and here we are. Thank you for accepting us. We may not be surprised if some follow us and join us too."

Introductions and understandings were achieved, and the next thing was to show them around the village and where to construct their houses.

The travelers settled well in the area. They built their houses and gardens and lived happily together.

The year after Papa accepted the first travellers into the village, more came. But this time, they were from different tribes. Papa had no choice but to accept them into the community. Just as before, I had friends to talk and play, but not so much as before. I was in my teenage and helping Papa was my primary role.

With many boys joining our fathers as warriors of the village, fighting strength increased even more than what fathers expected. Our fathers often asked us to travel the hunting zone and kept guard from traveling tribes invasion. On return, we checked our hunting traps and came home with some form of animal for meat.

Once, while on guarding duty, we sat together, and I asked each of them to account of their travel with their parents.

Singamai started."My father decided we leave the village because he had many brothers in the village. He looked beyond the horizon and saw huge unoccupied places and wanted to make a new settlement himself. He took the whole family and walked off one morning. We slept in the bush for several days and arrived here. Every time we climbed a hill, Father looked back to ensure the last village we lived is off sight. We moved further and ended here. 'Father doesn't want to continue further. That we stay with you and your papa."

"How do you feel staying here with us?" I asked.

"It is enjoyable, quiet, with no stories of migrating people fighting our people or among themselves." I thanked Singamai.

Watai had travelled from the coast. "My parents and I lived on the coast. One day Father took the whole family on his hunting trip. We travelled inland and along riverbanks and through bush tracks, Father and I were able to catch a lot of fish, birds, and other animals. At one place of rest on a riverbank, we stayed overnight, roasting meat. At midnight, a huge snake with head the size of coconut appeared. Perhaps it was attracted by the meat. Father had no choice but to kill it. We cut it up and roasted its meat in large flame.

"About midnight, the storm began. The trees almost fell on us. Lightning flashed, and thunder roared angrily above us. The place got so dark. We hurriedly moved the meat and other stuff into the wall-less shelter. We were safe from the rain but not cold and wind. Waves of wind blew one after the other. At one instant, the hard wind blew off our sheltered hut and moved us apart. Being so dark, we were unable to see each other.

"Then the wind blew us to unfamiliar location. Each of us kept to ourselves till daybreak. At dawn, daddy fetched us all unharmed except our roasted meat.

"The environment was unfamiliar. Daddy aimlessly led us through a track that eventually led to your village. Your father met us and allowed us to stay. I don't know how we got here or how to get back to the coast. Maybe one day we will go to my village on the coast."

"What's on the coast?" I asked.

"It is similar to this place, except it is flat and near the sea. There are many more fish than the number in the creeks and lakes here."

"Were there any new people travelling through your village?" I asked.

"Yes, but Daddy and his men chased them away." Watai answered. We all agreed that our fathers were strong men, and we be strong like them.

LAND SURVEY

The idea of sharing land came when Papa noticed the increasing number of tribal groups in the village. One evening, Papa said, "The village population will grow in future. We will need land for ourselves to hunt, fish, and build a garden. We will have to share the land around us. This is how it will be done. We will walk to those mountains and valleys, and divide the land among the five tribal groups.

"The division of land will follow the traditional guidelines of good moral standards based on our Melanesian customary principles. The first principle is come, first served. The first person to come becomes the primary landowner. However, although I was the first to settle here, I regard you all as primary landowners of the portions that will be shared in due time. This means we begin with five primary landowners."

Everyone cheered. One among the group mumbled, "What a great man with a humble, sharing, and serving heart."

Papa continued. "After this division, it will be your responsibility to share land with any later arrivals accepted into your group. They will become secondary landowners. Should those you accept take on another group or an individual from another tribe or clan, it is their responsibility to share part of their land and become tertiary landowners. Is this understood?"

The chorus answered, "Yes, great man, the information is clear."

The following day, the men travelled into the mountains. Papa led us to the top of the highest mountain, where we had a better view of the territory. Papa showed the area that would be divided and said, "From this mountain ridge to the other mountain and to where the sun sets is mine and will be for the Muruk tribe. The eastern side of the village, on my right, is for the other Muruk tribe that joined me. The land in front of me to the north is for the Eagle tribe. The southern part will be shared by the Snake and Fish tribes.

"The natural features that will separate land among groups will be mountaintops hilltops, rivers and creeks. They should divide the land between groups very well.

"Other features are huge trees and rocks.

We witnessed boundary lines and boundary posts that evening. The day was used up in naming places, rivers and creeks, marking boundary lines, and planting posts to show separation of land for ownership."Papa," I called, "I am hungry. Can we leave for home please?"

Papa knew everyone had the same concern. "Thank you, Bush. It's getting late, and we have to go. Thank you all for walking this far in drawing land boundaries for future generation ."

We walked home wearily."This was a hard work, wasn't it?" asked papa.

"Yes it was," one among the team answered.

"As the plan stands, the same job will be done next week on the eastern end of the territory." Papa ended the talk on the subject of the land survey. When we arrived home, had dinner and went to sleep early.

The next morning, Papa recall the method in land division and boundary features used. The man sitting next to papa announced, "Young men, the method you see today shall remain in for the future. Tribes or be custodian to the land, and be used collectively by its members.

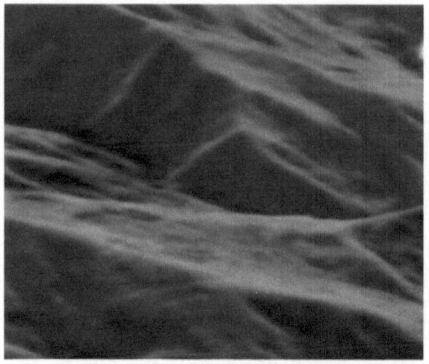

Hill tops, mountain ridges and rivers
used as land boundary features

SEETTING OF LAND OWNERSHIP PRINCIPLES

Rules of Law and Practices

After making permanent settlements and marking land boundaries, there came a time when guidelines were set and recorded in the memories of all men and women. "Bush," called Papa from the fireplace."

"I am listening, Papa."

"I have called a meeting for next month. All men in this village, the men living over those mountains and valleys, and those from the islands out in the sea will be coming here to make laws on landownership."

"Why all this? What will they eat?"

"Our lifestyle has changed. We no longer travel as we did some years ago. The population is growing, and all men will have to settle down in villages. In doing so, land is needed to hunt and make gardens. And many men and women will come to join us in the future, including your children when you grow big and get married. When the population increases, land will be scarce, and people will fight each other for it."

"Okay. That be a very good idea. What do I do?"

"You will need to help Mama gather some food and wood. The villagers will help too. The men will build extra shelters for sleeping, and the women will collect extra firewood and prepare food."

"Who do I help, Papa?"

"You will help the men with building shelters for the visitors."

The week Papa set for the preparation came. Papa signaled villagers through the garamut drum we had outside the house. I was still dreaming when it woke me up too. "Why hit the garamut so early? The people are still in bed," I asked from my bed.

"Ha, Bush. If you inherit my position as head of the village, you will have to lead. As such, you must wake up early, and others will follow."

Some hours later, the people came to our house, where there was talk about what to do prepare for the great day. Papa said, "Fellow villagers, we need to clean the village, construct new shelters, and cater some food."

I asked, "What will my friends and I do?"

"Thank you for asking, " Papa replied. "You will help the men build extra shelters and hunt for more meat. You will also help the women make sago. Starting tomorrow, all men will start collecting building materials and construct four shelters, one for every group of men who will be coming from all parts of the Melanesian territory. After that, we will hunt and store enough meat and food in these houses." The men understood what to do, and now it was the women's work. "The women will make sago with the boys' help, harvest yams from the gardens, and clean the village. In the evening, we will join in song and dance preparation until the day comes. The whole village—from children to the very elders—will help work till all is finished."

Several weeks were geared for this preparation. Men built houses for the travelling guests. They hunted, fished, and caught enough meat for themselves and the visiting guests.

The women, with the help of the male, harvested yams, prepared sago, and wood for fire. The village girls and the women cut grass, swept houses, and took care of the lawns.

Besides the day's work, the whole village also practiced songs and dances. All evening was taking up with singing and dancing. After several weeks of hard work, preparation was ready for the following special week. Messages sent to societies of nearby and distant villages to come the week after.

Some days before the scheduled week, the village chief and the great men from different Melanesian villages arrived. The first group was from the islands led by Toro. The second group, from the south, by Okoloko as chief. Yanga as chief from the west and Mushu from the north.

Papa greeted them and gave them shelter. They rested and went to sleep early, tired from the long travel.

The next morning, Papa visited the great guests. "How did you feel coming here?" Papa asked.

"My friend", replied Toro,"I was happy to be informed of your intention to set land law principles for our future generation. Although it was hard moving here, I made it through." The other great leaders and their men made same sentiment.

In each house prepared for them, there was plenty of food and wood for a fire. "Please, feel free to ask for anything. The food will be cooked and served to you by the women.But should you want more, cook more yourselves," said Papa.

The guests stayed for some days in the village before the starting date.

Very early the morning of the appointed day, garamut drums sounded the message that the meeting would start soon. "Bush," called Papa, "Uncle Watai will be waiting for you all in the rehearsal hut for the welcome dance. Getup quickly and meet him. He could be waiting for you there already."

I walked out of the house and rushed into the hut. Uncle Watai was there alone. "Uncle, may I use the conch shell to call the others over?"

"Of course," he replied and handed it to me.

"How do I blow it?"

"Ha, ha, son. I will show you how it is used." As he demonstrated, a *hoooo sound was produced*. Then he handed it to me. "Son, you try."

I did as shown but didn't get the sound out clearly. After several attempts, I managed to blow it well, and the *hoooo* echoed from one end of the village to the other. "Wow, I got it," I called to Uncle Watai.

"Yes, you did it." he said.

"My friend, your son, should be taught to use it," I told Uncle Watai.

"Yes, son. Maybe after the meeting."

Some minutes from my signal, the team of singers and dancers approached, and the rehearsal started. The day came with playing of the garamut drum, and dancing from the viilage women. Uncle Watai lead; the young boys and later, women and girls. The dance impressed everyone. To the guests, it was a warm welcome that they enjoyed a lot. The dance ended with excitement and the session commenced.

"Welcome, my friends, " started Papa."In brief, Melanesian history has taken us a long way to this date, We started as hunters and gatherers in search of food. We lived in temporary campsites in shelters make of twigs. We later travelled distant journeys, fighting among ourselves and tribal groups. And finally, we made the permanent settlement we are today. This will be our home and will shape future identities.

"Today's meeting is of great importance in the history of all Melanesians. Welcome once again, everyone." The crowds cheered with drumbeats and hand clapping. Papa continued while everyone who came listened with great attention. "The population and landownership will be an issue which will lead to fighting and killing among us. Therefore, the meeting here will outline some important basic land laws that will be practised in Melanesia.

"Several topics will be discussed at the meeting. The first topic is arranging the tribes in the sequence of their arrival. It will be presented by Mushu and his men from the east. My men and I will present a talk on the principles of land possession. Yanga and his men will present the topic on distribution. Toro and his men will speak about the categories of landownership. And finally, Okoloko and his men will take us into making laws that future generation will need to know and use in settling land arguments.

"Land distribution will consider time of arrival into an area as one aspect. Mushu and his great men from the east will lead us into this session. Please make them welcome. " said papa. The crowd beat drums and shouted cheerfully.

"Fellow Melanesians," Mushu started, "the sequence of migration from wandering lifestyle to a new way of life in establishing settlements has led us into possessing land. Population has increased and is a good reason to change lifestyle. History should keep evidence that travelling was done in groups—tribes and clans—in search of suitable settlement sites. This history should also be retold through stories and legends. It was the most difficult period in our lives. Fighting was used to clear travelling paths or conquer land from other tribes.

"Migrating tribal groups travelled in phases. There was the first migration group, second, third group, and more. Mountaintops and hilltops were often used as settlement sites as they provided secure locations for defense against other travellers. Lower land areas were used for hunting and food-gathering to sustain life.

"The tribal fighting consequentially resulted in the losing group fleeing to a new location, while the winning team occupied its territory. Irrespective of where these groups moved, those clans or tribal groups that decided to establish make permanent settlements on certain land territories become primary landowners.

The second and third flocks of travelers had no opportunities to occupy their own lands. They continued on to uninhabited lands and became primary landowners, or they were asked to stay with the first settlers and share land. This made them secondary or tertiary landowners.

The final destination point of the travelling period and the first permanent settlement ever made by ancestors opened the first chapter to the story of land, which many Melanesians call 'my traditional land.'

"To help understand this concept, we will get into our village groups and list the tribes or clans in the order of their arrival."

"Bush," Papa called, "list the tribes in our village in the order of their arrival."

"Okay, Papa."

The discussions and listings went on for an hour. In our group, we listed the tribes in this order:Muruk 1, Muruk 2, Tarangau, Snake, and Fish.

Mushu explained."I will use Malaka's village as an example. Malaka is the chief of hosting village, and he has five tribes:Muruk 1, Muruk 2,Tarangau, Snake, and Fish. Muruk 1 arrived first, followed by Muruk 2.Then came the Tarangau tribe and the Snake. The most recently arrived tribe is the Fish. The first group, Muruk 1,is the primary landowners. The others secondary owners. Is this understood?"

"Yes, great man from the east," responded the crowd, and the session ended. The people had a break for the second part.

After break, the second session begin. "Please come, The second session is about to start. My men and I will outline the principles of landownership. Six methods will be discussed." announced Papa.

"The first method is pioneership. This was discussed earlier by Mushu. The pioneership method refers to those undefeated tribes that made the first settlements on land. Occupation of land by these first settlers shall be deemed as primary landowners.

"The second mode of landownership is obtained through fighting. This is the method in which original owners were chased away or killed in a battle, and the land was taken over by successive groups. When the first wave of travellers is forced out and driven into distance land, sea, and islands, the new arrivals occupied the land. The warfare method involved collective efforts from many tribe members, villages, and societies. The land therefore had to be divided evenly among the involved tribal groups. This situation can allow them to become primary owners.

In another situation, the warrior who kills an enemy is rewarded for his bravery. For example, Waresu, a member of Muruk tribe, killed Mangamba, an enemy warrior. The land area where the killing took place is owned by members of the Muruk tribe. On the other, if the enemy killed Waresu, the

Muruk clan has some rights to ownership of the site where the body was shot as a means of compensation for the life lost.

"In such situations, all involved tribes possess almost the same amount of land. They share same tribal history and line of generation. They can be categorised as secondary owners."

"The third method of landownership is what I call leniency method," said Malaka. "This is the method which a portion of land is shared with relatives of late migration groups.

The travelling period was a hazardous time. It was a do-or-die game. It meant winning the fight, surviving, and owning the land, or fleeing and losing the landownership title. Stories are told in many societies that some clans or tribes were totally annihilated through tribal fighting. The few children or men found were adopted into other tribes that had land shared and became secondary landowners."

Papa continued."The fourth method shall be an ownership through an agreement deal of exchange method. Land shall be owned through exchange for possession or other approved deals."

"Can you explain further, please?" a man from the crowd asked.

"Thank you," Papa continued."This is the method in which a land title can be exchanged from one tribe to another through material giving as means of price. Such traditional monies can be used to pay for the land."

"What is the other?" asked a young man.

"Due to fragmentation of land, some tribes may own land that is too far away to travel to do gardening and hunting. They can create a deal in which the title is exchanged with another tribe with more easily accessible land.

"This should be clearer with this explanation. Let's take two tribes, the Muruk and Kurum, for example. Assume the

Muruk tribe owns a piece of land seven kilometres from their village location and near the Kurum tribal village.Kurum has a similarly sized piece of land within easy travelling distance from the Muruk tribe's village. On agreement, the two land parcels can be exchanged and ownership title changed. The tribe living next to the land owns it and vice versa. This is done solely due to not wanting to travel a far distance. I hope this explanation is clear," Papa concluded.

"Is there anymore to be said?" asked an old man.

"Yes, please, the fifth method, which land is used as material for exchange in honour for debt deem worthy in the custom. This is the process by which landownership can be transferred in exchange for completing a task valued as important in each culture. Land shares can be given to individuals society may deem worthy of rewarding. Some of these practices include adaptation of child to manhood from other tribes or village, taking care of deceased person by non-relatives, and offering large pieces of slaughtered pig meat to neighbour. These are examples of valued customs in Melanesian societies. In the act of doing these actions, land can be given as prize.

"The final method that must be upheld in the custom is that of over-righting.This is the method by which tribe members die, and the land title is transferred to others. In other words, the initial owners die without male offspring in a patriarchal society or female offspring in a matriarchal society to continue the line of generation and extended family members claiming the land.

In a patriarchal ownership system, a sister shall have right to a land title over what was to go to her father. In a matriarchal society, women have traditional rights to own her mother's land when she dies. However, if there is no sister to carry on the leadership, the brothers shall take over the land title.

"All that I have presented shall be practiced in all Melanesian society and kept in custom for future generations" said Papa."But before I sit down, let me summarise the six methods.

1. Pioneer ship
2. Fighting method
3. Leniency method
4. Exchange method
5. Prize-offering method
6. Over-right custom"

Having summarised his talk, Papa sat down. He thanked his team members for their presentations about the important basic landownership laws in Melanesia. Then the drums were played and songs sung to end the first day's meeting.

"The third session will outline how land was shared among the tribal groups in a society. Mushu and Malaka have discussed most of my talk and explanation," said Yanga. "History must reveal that our fathers became wanderers and later settled in villages we would call home-developed. The travelling fathers moved far distances in search of suitable land. The land where we choose to settle today is what we now call, 'my land,' and it will shape our generations' identity.

"The first groups of people were strong, undefeated tribes who decided to travel no more. The other groups were relatives of first settlers and were asked to end their journeys and stay permanently with them. Others were looked after as orphans as a result of tribal fighting or reasons that may differ from society to society.

"The land which Melanesian people will claim as traditional land was the final settlement site of their ancestors.Names tags were given to identify land sites. These names were taken from the first settler, a great warrior, common natural feature of the environment, or something else, depending on interest of tribesmen and tribes women. More important, the naming of land verified an event that once occurred on that land.

"Land was further divided and distributed among the members as the number of migrants increased. Various criteria were applied in the sharing of the land. Apart from those who first settled as surveyors of the land, portions of land were given to late arrivals, great warriors, as a reward to deceased warriors, bride's price, and exchanged for customary value practices.

"Yanga is done. Can we have Toro and your men from the islands?" called Papa.

Toro said, "Gentlemen and women from this region, I have come a long way across the sea to share with other Melanesian the landownership principles our future generation shall have to work the land we now occupy. I wish to thank Malaka for the initiative taken. Thank you very much. Now I will proceed with my session.

"The methods and criteria used in showing landownership in Melanesia shall be practiced in the customs of each society. Most customs have similar methods but may differ in one or two cases conducive to the surrounding environment.

"In fact, there is a primary landowner—PLO—a secondary landowner—SLO—and a tertiary landowner—TLO. Division can be extended to fourth and fifth owners.

"The PLO are those tribes or clans who were the first people to settle on the land. These tribes later shared portions of their land with others who later joined them. The tribes identified as primary owners of most traditional land are those who have historical records of owning the last portion of land, looked after other tribes, shared part of their land territory, and have existed longer than other tribes in a society."

"Who are secondary landowners?" asked a man in the crowd.

"The secondary landowners—SLO—are those tribes with whom sister tribes, usually primary landowners, shared land. These groups were the second flow of migrants travelling in search of land to settle. The SLO can be identified by shared land boundaries with the sister primary clan. They also participate with primary clan members in such culturally organized activities as festivals and ceremonies.

"The TLO were given portions of land by the secondary landowners in honour of duty displayed according to customary practices considered valuable."

"Can you give an example please?" asked Watai.

"Sure. For example, if members from Eagle tribe hospitalized a sick person from the Frog tribe, on death of this man, the Frog tribe may give a portion of its land to Eagle tribe in thanks for the care given and cost accrued in the hospitalization of the patient. Eagle tribe now becomes a secondary landowner of the land portion given by the Frog tribe if it was the primary owner. If Frog tribe was a secondary owner, the Eagle tribe becomes a tertiary owner of that land."

"Thank you. The explanation is very clear," said Watai.

"Before I conclude, I wish to contribute another important matter that needs understanding and be kept as custom in relation to land matters. We used rivers, creeks, mountains, and hill ridges indicate boundaries of land. I call these boundary lines.

"Another term, 'boundary post', include features as huge trees and stones.

"All land sites shall have names. Other speakers have addressed how these names are chosen. Perhaps most important is for these names to have a common understanding among all Melanesians today and in future."

"Now we come to the final session. Okoloko will take us into writing the rules for landownership in Melanesia," said Malaka.

Okoloko began his part of the session. "Ladies and gentlemen, today we have to make the most important part of landownership principles in Melanesia. That is, to set laws for future generation to use in determining how land is owned, who has rights over land titles, and who does not have customary rights. I will term these the 'Commandments of Melanesian Landownership.' It summarises all that's been discussed by other men."

"I made the first outline of primary ownership," said Mushu. "Thank you. The following shall be rules of law in Melanesia.

1. A tribe shall have right to a landownership title if its ancestors were the first migration groups that made permanent settlement on the occupied land and be considered primary landowners.

2. The clan or tribe shall have right to a landownership title if their ancestors participated in a tribal war and killed an enemy warrior or was killed on the land site and be considered secondary or primary otherwise.

3. The tribe or clan shall have right to landownership title if an ancestor received a titled transfer from a sister clan and became a secondary owner. The tribe or clan under this category shall pay wealth in form of food and traditional money to the primary holders.

4. The tribe or clan shall have rights to a landownership title if the title is transferred to another in exchange

for a traditional obligation; it becomes a secondary or tertiary owner.

5. The woman shall have right to a landownership title if the male offspring in the tribe or clan have died in a patriarchal society that maintains that family principle.

6. In societies where women are heads of the tribe and land title ownership, they also become custodians to traditional land rights. The man shall have ownership to land on the death of the sister(s)."

It was getting late in the evening when the session ended. Papa was tired and asked Watai to help out with the next task of instruction for the evening.

"I understand everyone is tired and needs rest," Watai commented. "Please have shower and return to your rest house. To our guests, the women will serve your dinner. And please have a good sleep tonight."

Papa whispered to Watai. "The hosting chief wants our guests and the public to know there will be a feast tomorrow. The feast is his token of appreciation for the hard work done by the community and the guests. Is this clear to all?"

"Yes, please," they responded.

"Go and have rest. The meeting is over," announced Watai, and the crowd began to leave. A few people stayed longer, but the night was so quiet, many went to bed early.

FAREWELL

Papa had decided the meetings would end with a farewell feast, a thanksgiving meal to the villagers for their hard work in the preparation, management, and participation in the week's meeting. Several pigs and cassowaries would be killed and served with vegetables.

Early the next morning, Papa rang the garamut, and people gathered food in preparation for the feast. Some men and boys killed and roasted the pigs. I went with some other men and killed cassowaries. It was not easy to do so with simple spears. But we managed to kill them all and brought them for slaughtering and roasting.

The mothers cooked yams, sago, bananas, and taro. By midday, the other boys and I felt we needed lunch. Mama, who was very busy, noticed us and led us to a meal of taro and pork.

After the meal, we walked about the village and watched groups of village men and women prepare food their ways. Some cooked food in clay pots, and some cooked foods wrapped in leaves. Some were cooking on fires, while others placed parcels on a hot stone.

While the food was cooking, people sat under coconut trees, chewing betel nuts, chatting, and cracking jokes.

"Hey guys, can we go and talk to some of our guests?" I asked.

"Who do we talk to, Bush?" Singamai asked.

"The yellow-haired man," I replied. I walked over to him and the others sitting in a shade of a mango tree.

"Hallow," I greeted him. "I am Bush, the village chief's son. These are my friends, sons of other men in the village."

"Good young boys, you are strong like your fathers. I am Toro," he said, and the boys smiled.

"You are different from most of us. I mean, you have yellow hair. How did that come about. Did you use paints?" I asked.

He laughed and then explained. "This is the natural human feature of the people on the island. Most people have yellow hair and are as tall as your father. Some are black as charcoal from the fire. But none of them came to the meeting because of the distance by sea."

"This is interesting," said the curious boys.

"Okay, great Toro, what other color people do we have on this land?" I asked.

"There are brown people, black people, light people, and white people. We are brown and black in Melanesia. White and light-skin people live outside this land," explained Toro.

"How will you go home?" asked Singamai.

"Son, it will take us several days to travel. We will walk up and down mountains to the sea and then jump in a canoe. That will take some weeks too," Toro answered. We boys decided to convince Papa to give Toro's group enough food to take. We thanked Toro for his time and left.

Late in the afternoon, the food was ready and brought to the public area. The food was shared equally among the guests and villagers. The other boys and I assisted.

Before eating, Papa called everyone together for the farewell message. "I wish to thank the four chiefs for coming this far to attend the week-long meeting. You all have contributed a lot in what will remain in Melanesian history as the truth of landownership principles.

"I wish to offer you the first share of the meal. Please come and take your share as distributed."

"Thank you, great man," they responded and took their shares.

"Now, I wish to thank my own good people of this village. You have worked so hard in making the meeting a great success. Please take your share of food, and eat till satisfaction."

Finally, he added, "Singsing will commence tonight. I wish you all happy eating, and enjoy dancing." Having said this, the people got their food and moved to their houses.

At night, everyone danced to the rhythmic beat of the drums, the colorful tunes, and dancing pattern. The dance went until daybreak.

The guests rested for another day and then travelled home with our farewells and food for the days before they reached their homes.

"Ayo, ayo, ayo," was our farewell as the great people left the village. Over the hills and mountains, rivers and sea they travelled. Over the horizons they went. And that was it.

SUMMARY

Historical Perspective of Melanesian Land and Ownership

Most Melanesian people lived a life as wanderers and food-gatherers. Later they established permanent settlements. In those early days, they had neither land nor homes. Modern literature cites evidence found in Papua New Guinea to place the existence of human beings in New Guinea fifty thousand years ago. However, settling down in homes as benchmarks to landownership was not achieved until very late in AD 1000.

There were three historical periods of movement. There were a wandering period, a travelling period, and a selection of land sites period.

The Wandering Period

The wandering period occurred when people moved from place to place in search of food. According to most scholars, the people were hunters, fishermen, and those who gathered wild plants for food. There was nothing for them as a home, garden, village, or land. This was the longest time of events which Melanesian traditional history can't recall.

While the earliest evidence of human occupation fifty thousand years ago, the first sign of gardening in the highlands area (settlement period) was nine thousand years ago. For these few groups in the highlands, they spent thirty-five thousand years as wanderers before making their first permanent settlements.

For many groups, it took many years as wanderers before establishing permanent settlements. However, what could be kept as legend can only be traced to the last hundreds of years. The land remained no man's property in those times.

The Travelling Period

This was the time when early ancestors ended the wandering lifestyle for a new way of life, making settlements. Population increase may have been a possible cause of this changing lifestyle.

According to some village historical stories/legends, and some local oral history has confirmed, travelling was done in groups as tribes and clans. They travelled in search of suitable settlement sites. There was heavy fighting among travelling clans and tribal groups. Fighting was used to clear travelling pathways or conquer land from other tribes.

Mountains and hilltops were often used as sites for settlement as they provided effective locations for defense. Lower land areas were used for hunting and food-gathering to sustain life.

Travelers also obtained land as a result of fighting among different groups. The losing group would flee to a new location, leaving the winning group to occupy its territory.

Irrespective of where these groups moved, those clan or tribal groups that decided to make permanent settlements became primary landowners of today's society.

The next (second/third) flock of travelers had no opportunities to occupy their own lands. They continued on to uninhabited land and became primary landowners there. Or they were asked to stay back with the first settlers and shared their land, making the latter travelers secondary or tertiary landowners.

The final destination point of the travelling period and the first permanent settlement made by the ancestors opens the first chapter to the story of land many Melanesians now call "my traditional land". To date, a good number of clan groups can recall names of ancestors, events, and happenings back to the tenth, or the furthest, to the twentieth generation.

The Settlement Period

A time came when the idea of settling down in villages, or what we would call having a permanent home, developed. And the travelling ancestors moved far distances in search of suitable land.

The first groups of people were those strong, undefeated tribes who decided to travel no more because they found a suitable site or couldn't move further. The other groups were relatives of first settlers and were asked to end their journeys and stay permanently with them. Others were looked after as orphans due to tribal warfare or other reasons that may differ from society to society. The land which Melanesian people today claim as traditional land is the final settlement site of their ancestors.

Land Identity

Names tags were given to identify land sites. These names were taken from the first settler, great warrior, common natural feature of the environment, or other means depending on the interest of the tribesmen and tribeswomen. More important, the naming of land verifies an event that occurred on that land.

Land was further divided and distributed among the members as the numbers of migrants increased. Various criteria were applied in the sharing of the land. Apart from those who first settled as surveyors of the land, a portion of land was given to late arrivals, great warriors, as a reward to a deceased warrior, a bride's price, an exchanged, and customary value practices. They become primary evidence to justify arguments about land ownership. These are orally recorded or otherwise practiced in Melanesian customs.

Six common methods are practiced in most Melanesian societies. Landownership title is rightly given to a clan group based on the following conditions and acts.

1. Survey method (applicable to only PLO)
2. Warfare method (SLO/PLO)
3. Leniency method (SLO/TLO)

4. Exchange method (SLO/TLO)

5. Honor of customary values method (SLO)

6. Extinction method.

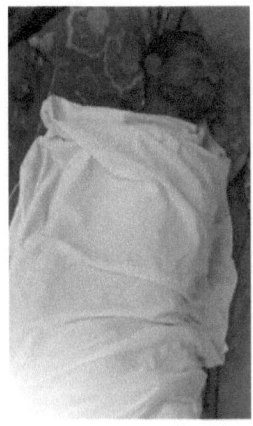

Land Boundaries

Traditional land boundaries are marked by rivers, creeks, ridges, and trees. On coastal and island societies rocks, swamps and trees and features.

GLOSSARY

Ayo: Goodbye.
Belhat: The act of being annoyed.
Garamut: A carved wooden drum.
Singsing: A singing and dancing ceremony.
Tanget: A plant often used to mark land boundaries in Melanesia.
Ware: Breadfruit

ABBREVIATIONS

PLO: Primary landowner
SLO. Secondary landowner
TLO. Tertiary landowner

EXTRA PICTURES